Elia Guarneri Silvino
Black Wolf Edition

Technical Lessons

(Based on passages taken from Sonatas and Concertos)

First Lesson

from

-LA FLUTE DE PAN Op. 15-

Pan et les Oiseaux

(Jules Mouquet)

© 2016 Black Wolf Edition & Publishing Ltd.

Copyrighted Work by:
Patamù
Opera filed on: 13 August 2015
Register No.23229
License type: All rights reserved

ISBN: 978-1-911424-09-3
ISMN: 979-0-9002358-3-1

SKU/ID: 9781911424093

Publishing Company:
Black Wolf Edition & Publishing Ltd..
2 Glebe Place Burntisland KY3 0ES, Scotland
www.blackwolfedition.com

Copyright © 2016 by Black Wolf Edition & Publishing Ltd.
All rights reserved. - First Printing: 2016

TECHNICAL LESSONS
(Based on passages taken from Sonatas and Concertos)

Elia Guarneri Silvino
(1973)

1st Lesson
EXCERPTS from - La Flute de Pan "Pan and the Birds" (Mouquet J.)

All this lesson has to be studied slowly to reach gradually the speed of ♩=100 for all the exercises; ♩=76 for the Study; ♩=63 for the final exercise.
It would be useful to practice the study in sections as it is divided. The student has to take in consideration and to work also on clean sound - deep but not pushed/heavy - on pitch, rhythm, right posture and fingers' position without forgetting to breath at the end of every phrase avoiding breaking the melodic line.

Enjoy the practice time!

Elia Guarneri Silvino

Exercise A

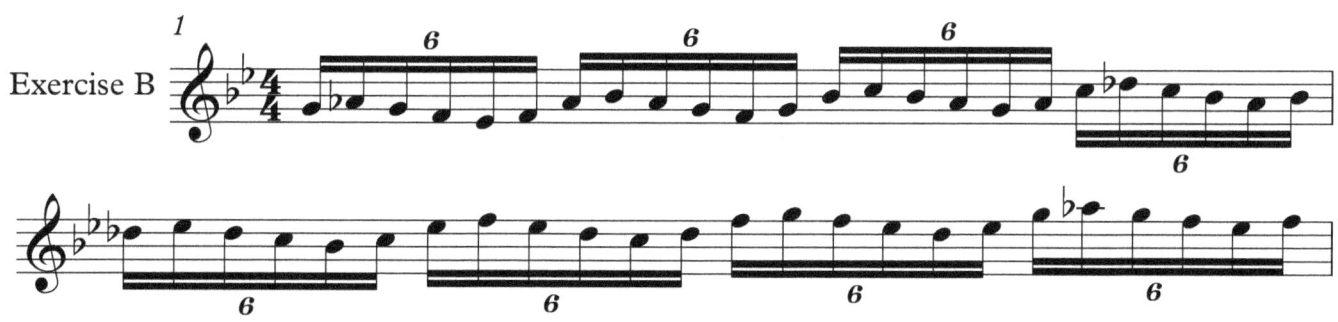

Exercise B

© 2016 Black Wolf Edition & Publishing Ltd.

Study

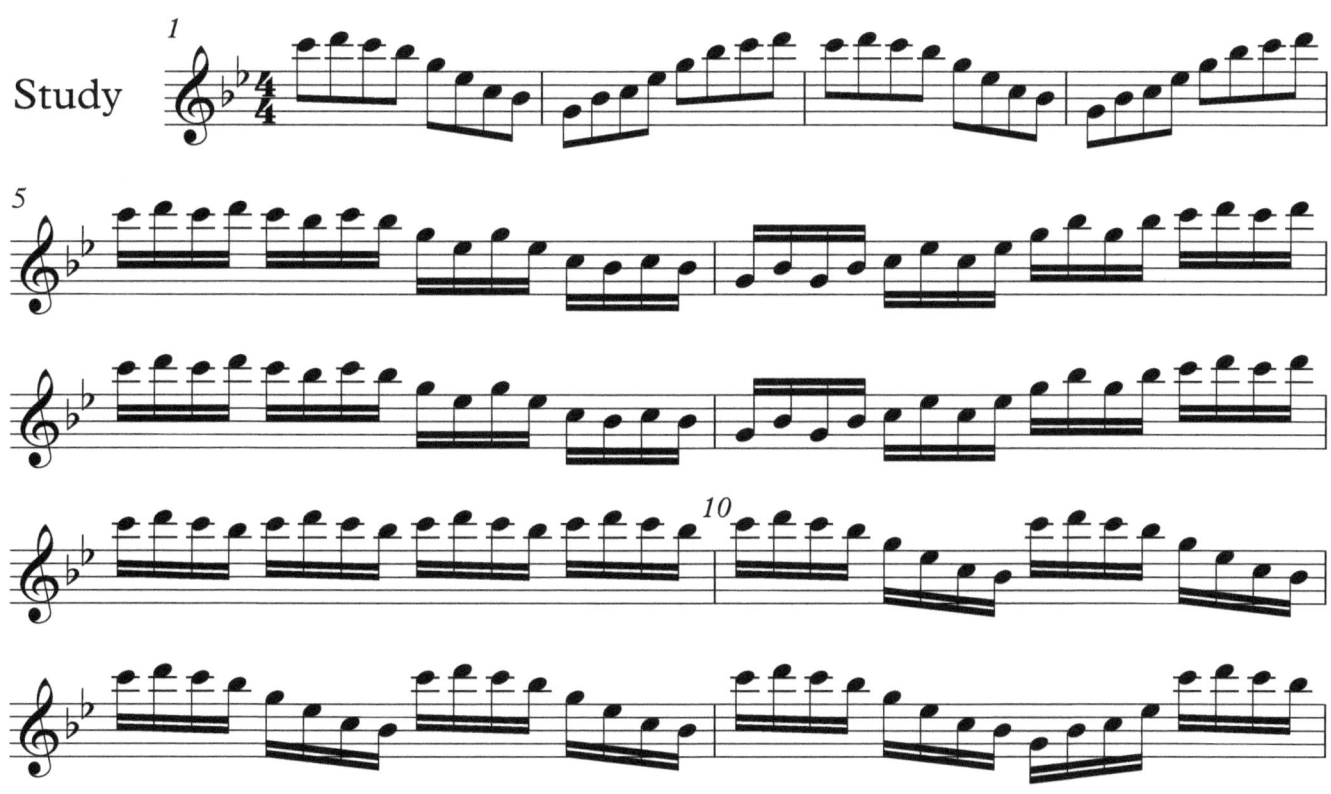

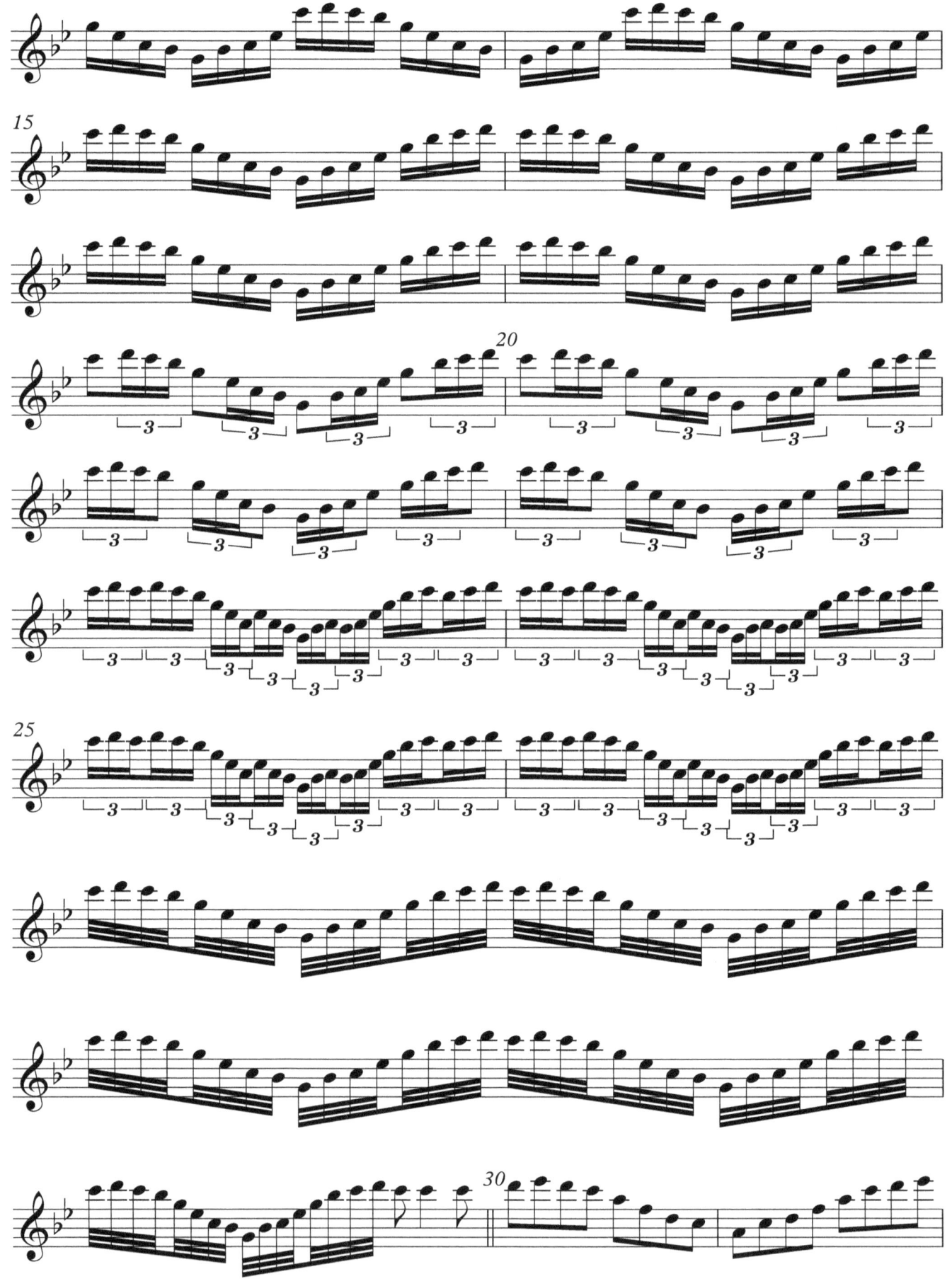

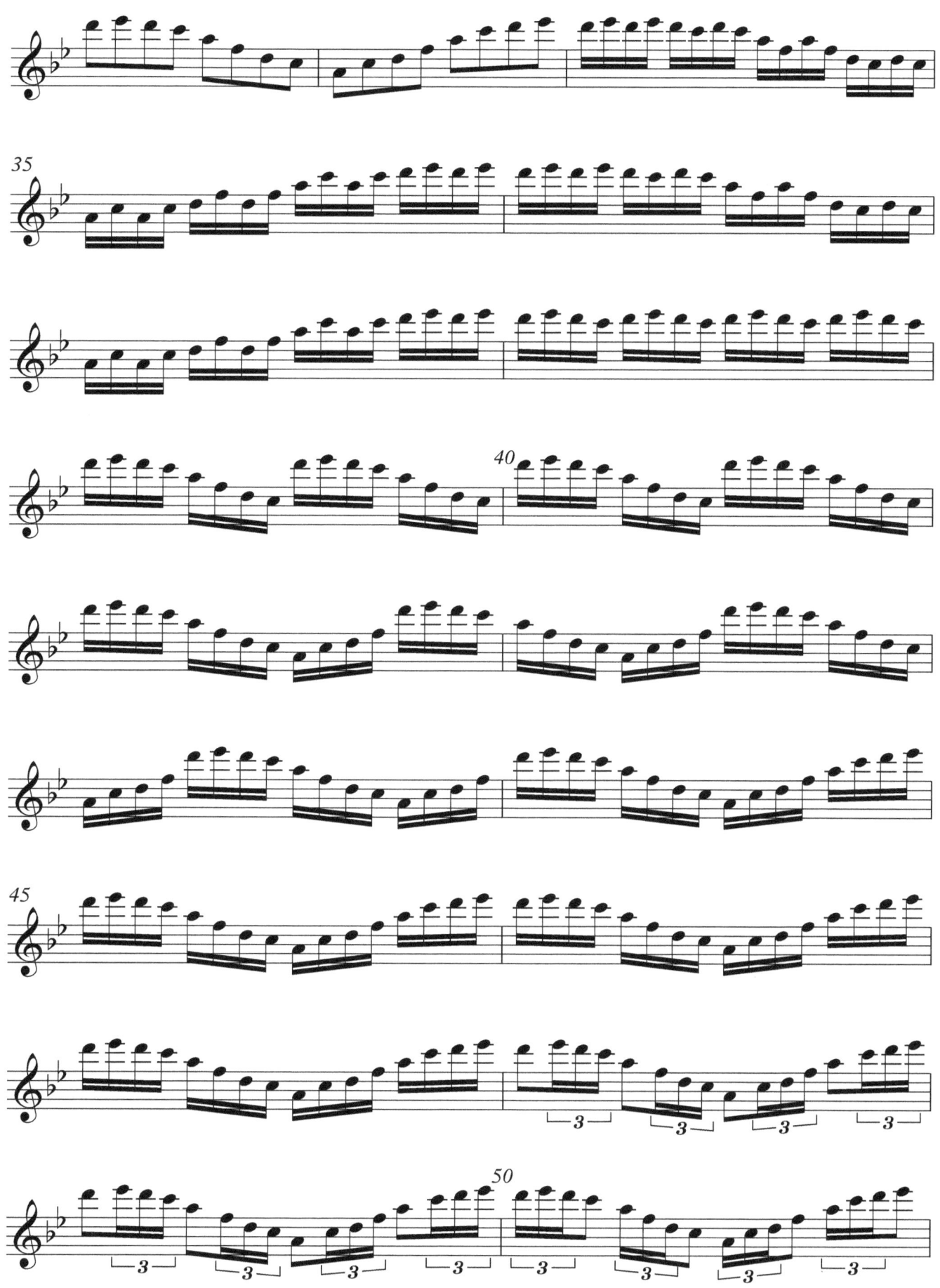

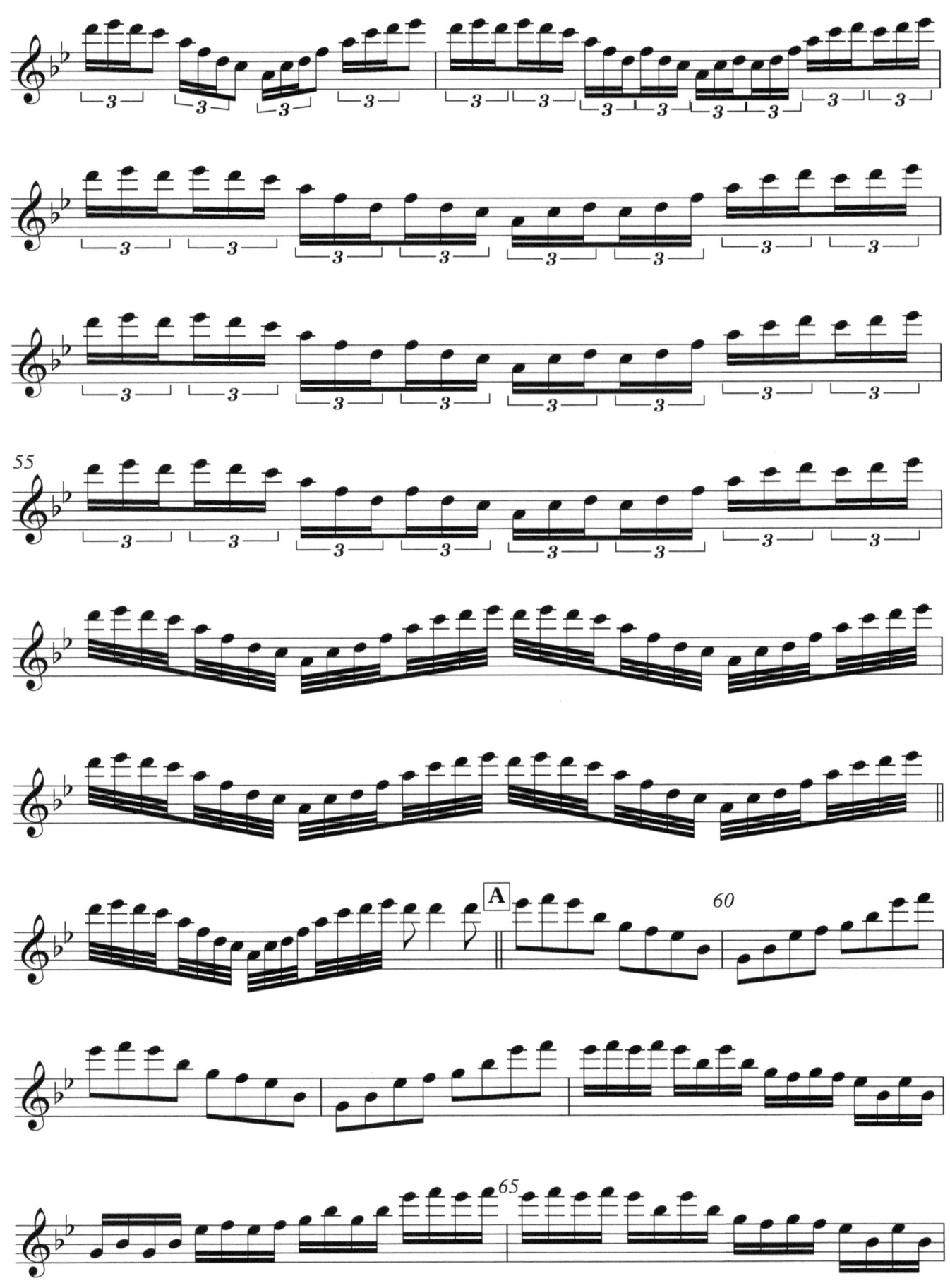

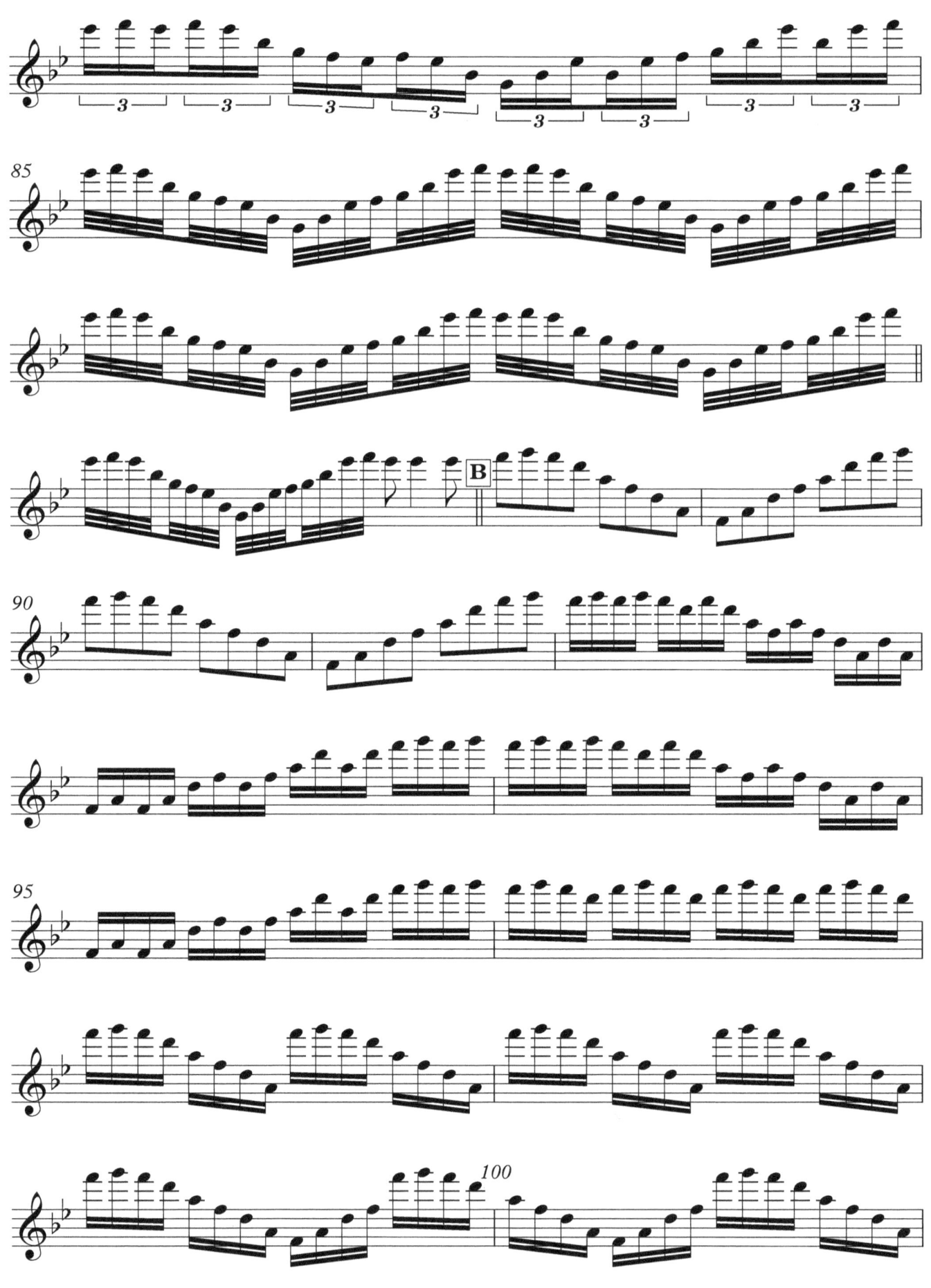

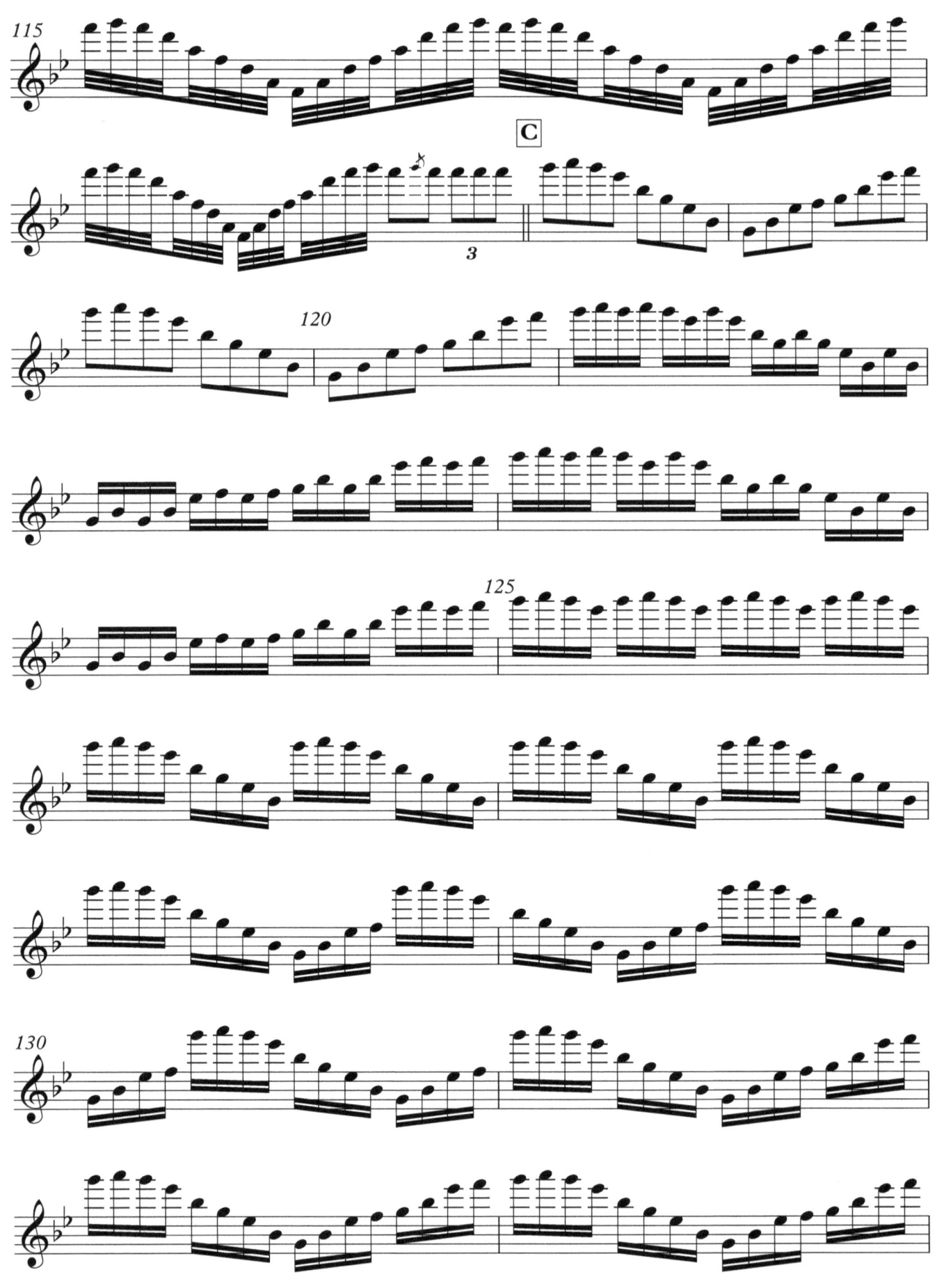

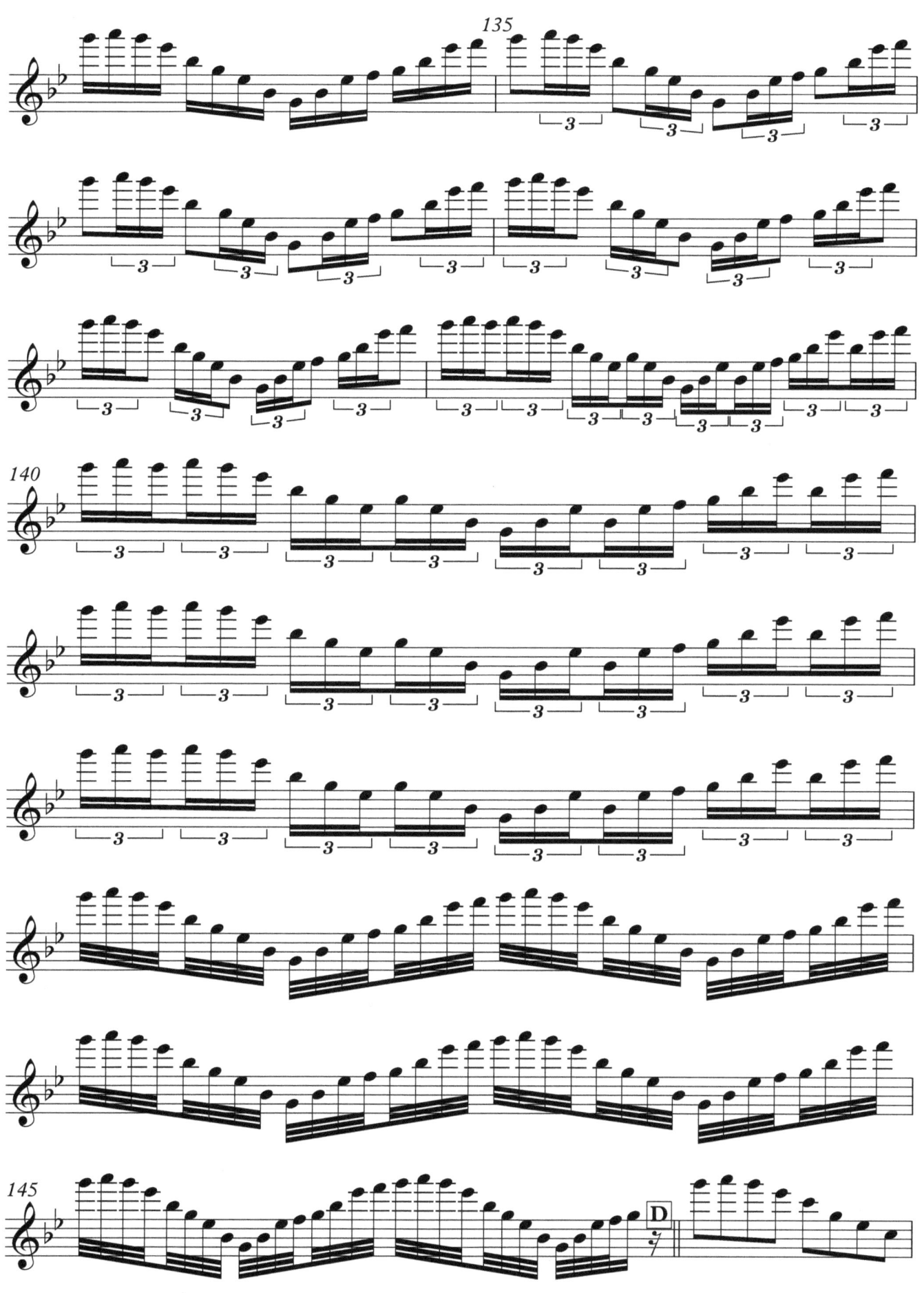

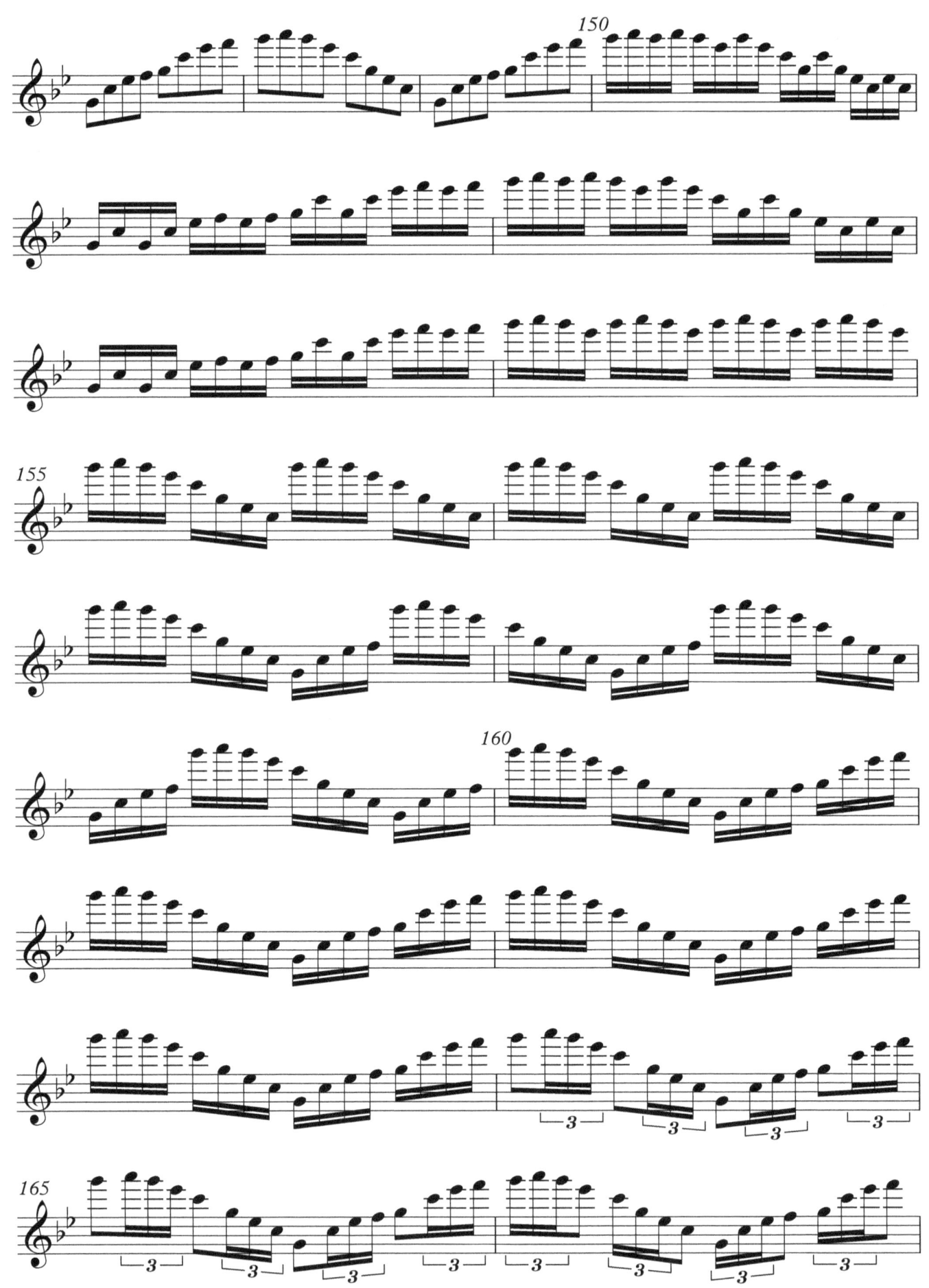

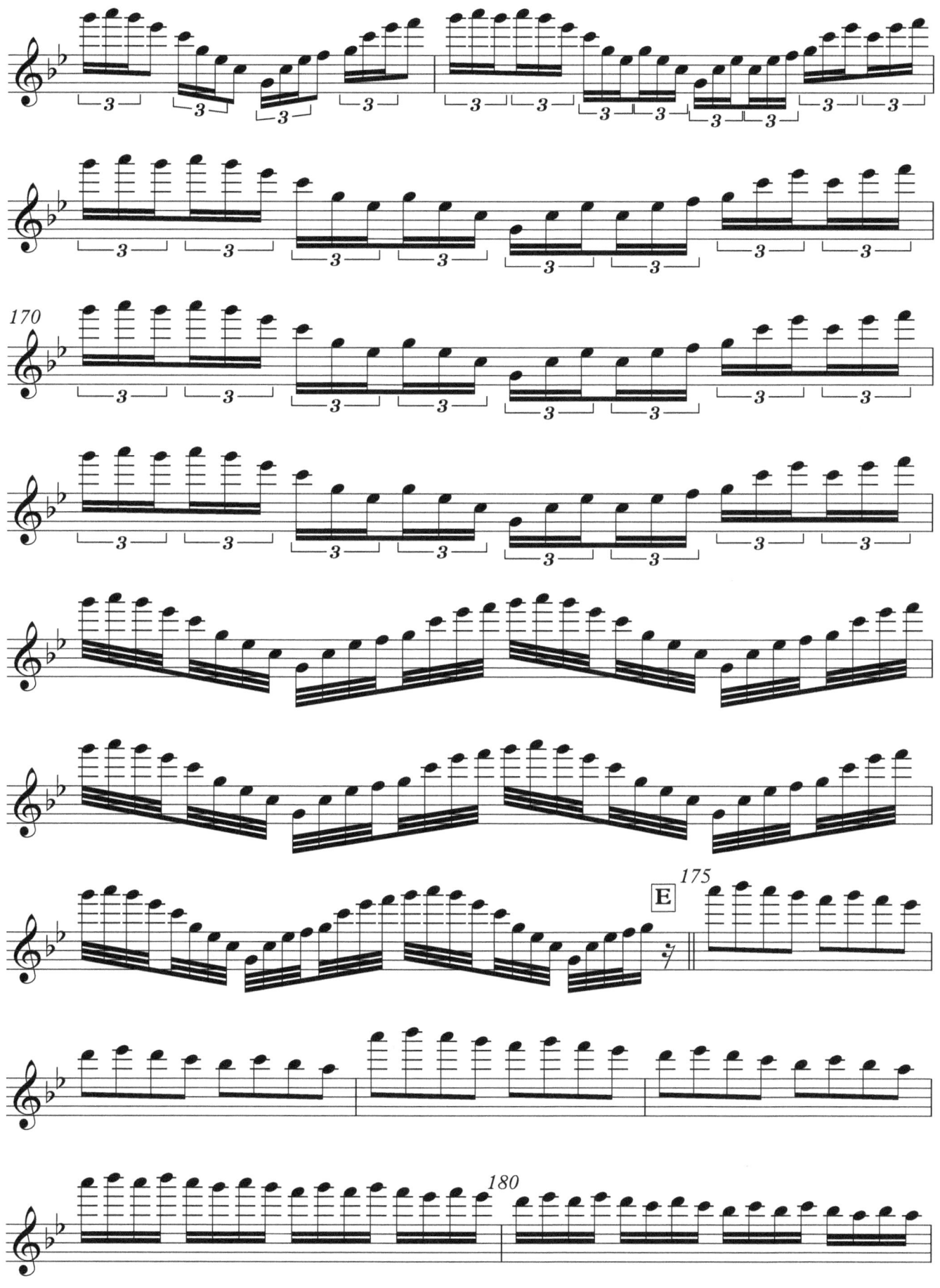

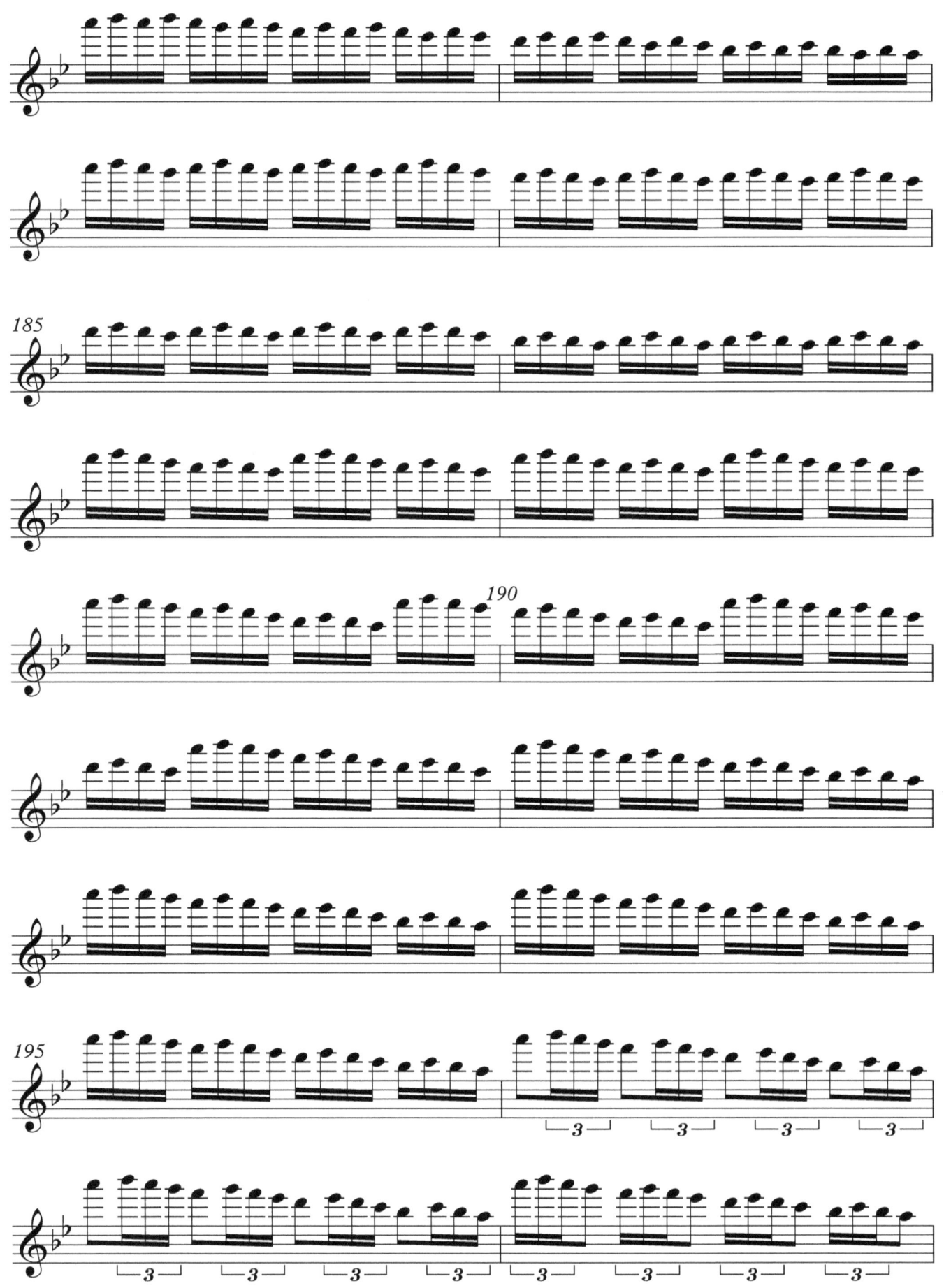

17

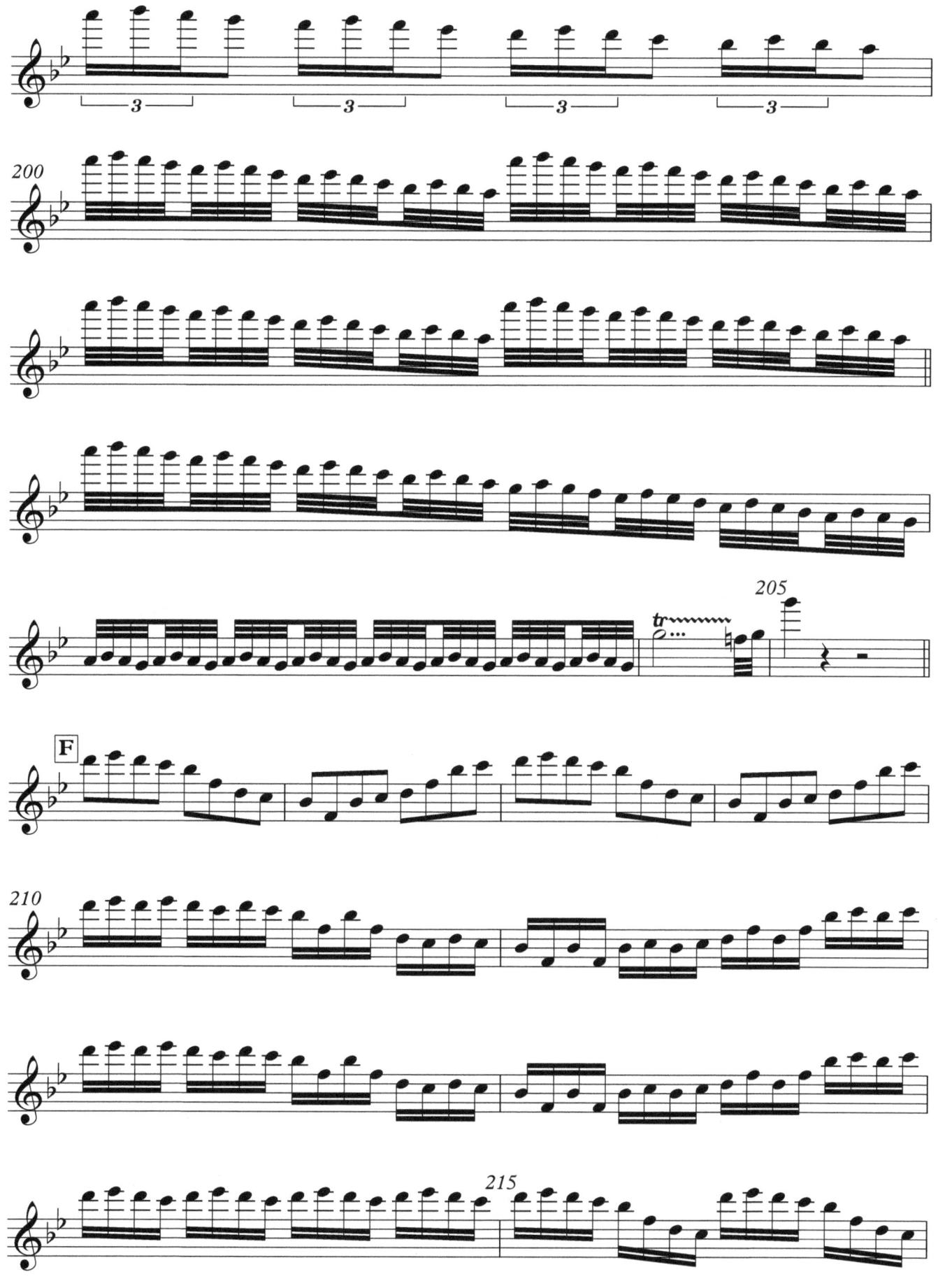

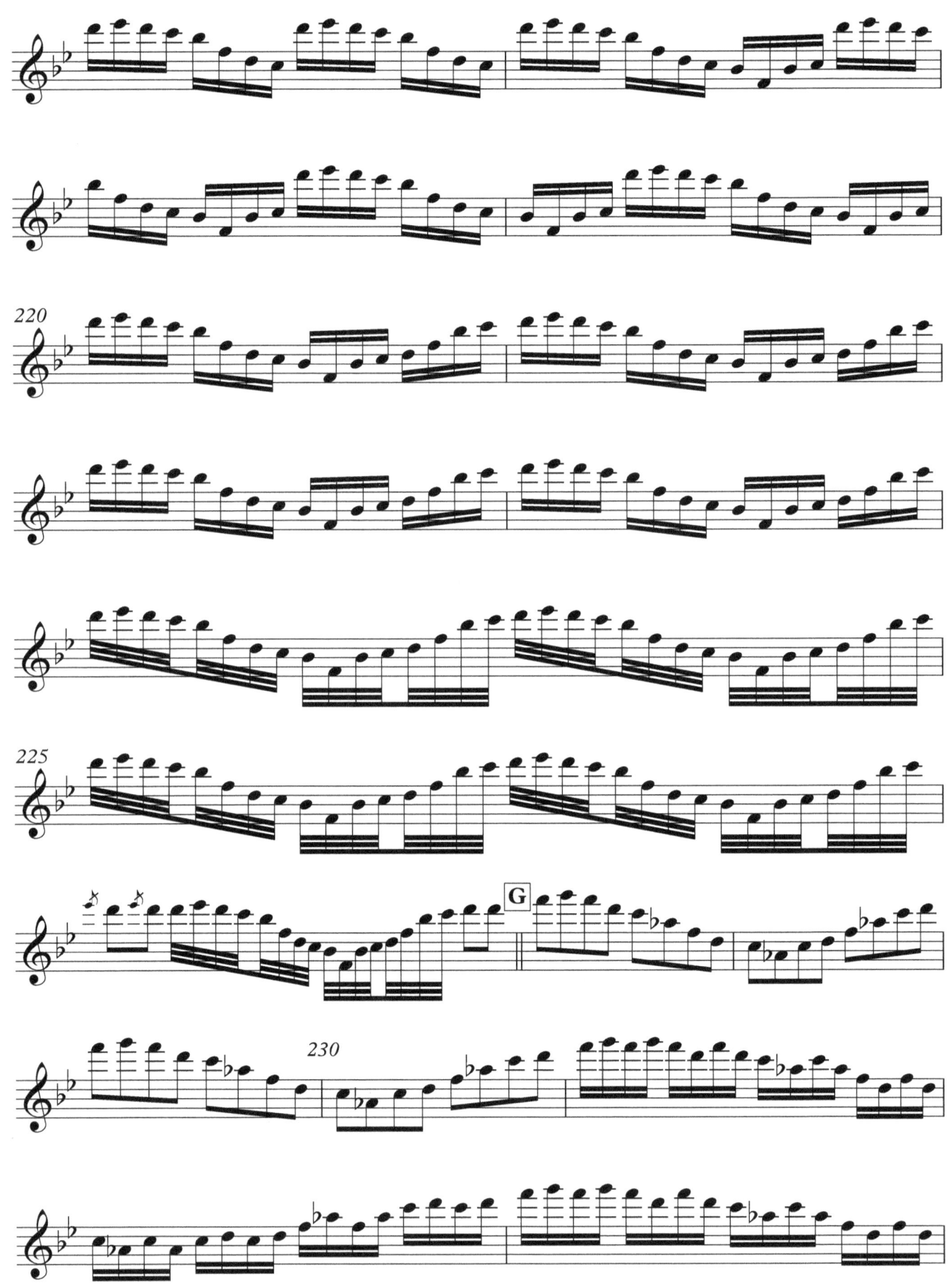

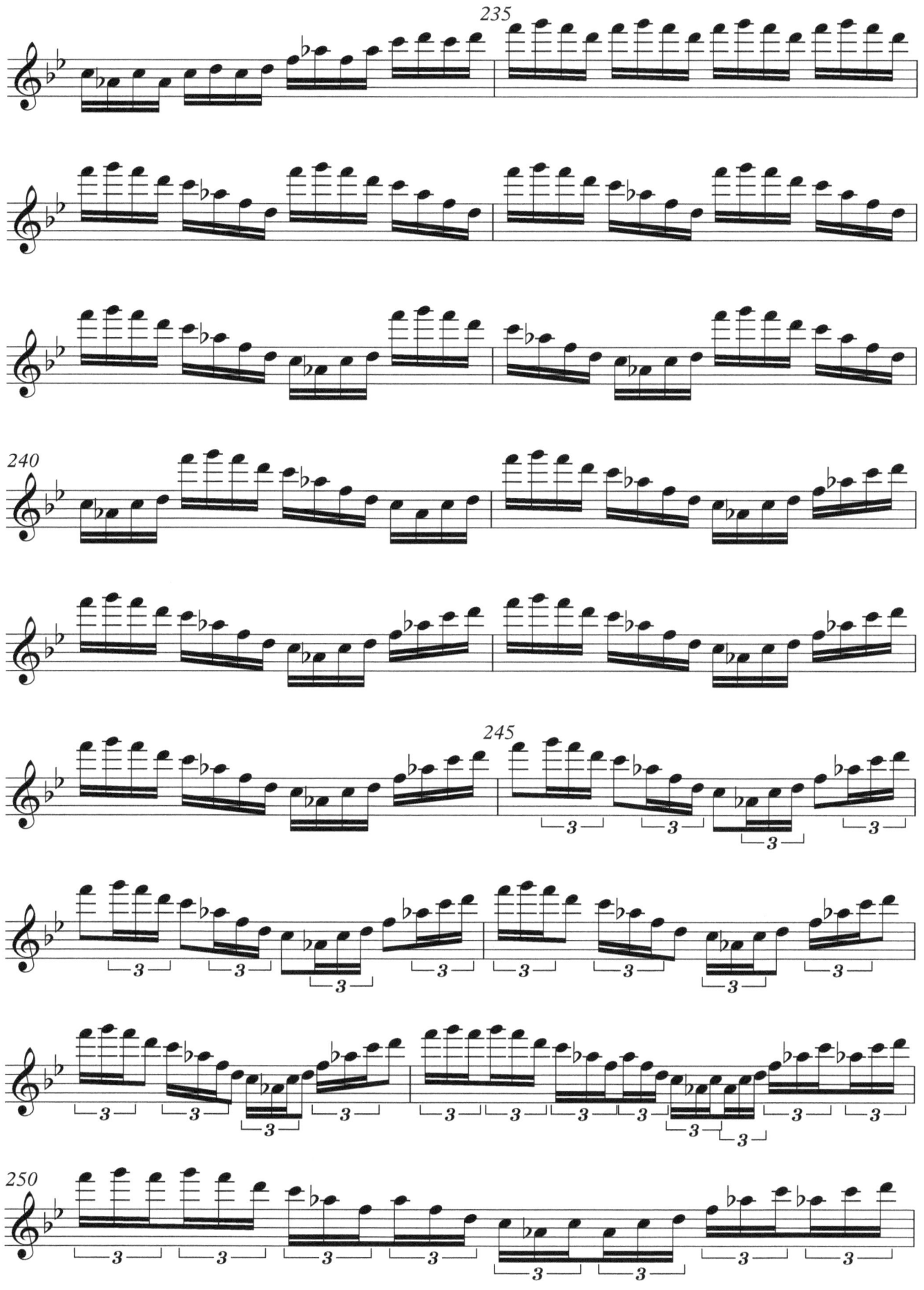

EXCERPTS from - La Flute de Pan "Pan and the Birds" -

Note - Notes

"KAKULIN STONE series SS is THE BEST FLUTE!

The production and manufacture of this flute is treated carefully.
Only by playing it you realise that is a good flute. It has a soft, excellent sound in all its registers.
I am proud to play with this flute."

(Elia Guarneri Silvino)

KAKULIN
WWW.KAKULIN.NET
TAIWAN

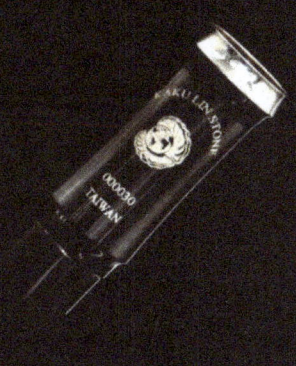

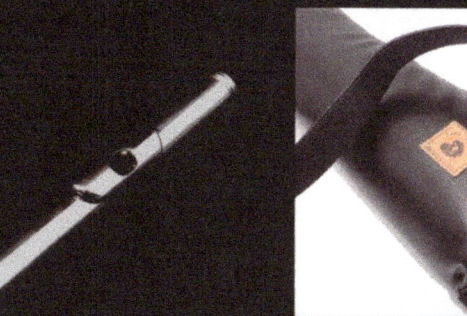

STONE Series SS

1. Handcrafted mold for the keys featuring ergonomic design makes it easy to play and reduces injury.
2. The new design of the barrel centralizes the energy of the sound, effectively conveying the sound to the body tube.
3. Thickened silver-plating offers more protection for the tube and elevates the sound quality.
4. One-piece key cups : The one-piece key cup provides superior strength and a neater appearance than traditional key cups.

Description
A=442
Nickel silver Body - Silver Plating (t=12μ)
925 Silver Head joint
Nickel silver Key Material - Silver Plating (t=12μ)
E Mechanism
Low B Foot joint
Drawn Tone Holes
Open Holes
Offset G Key System
Stainless Spring

Instrument Assembly Set
A: Accessory Envelope
B: Guarantee of Quality
C: Accessory Envelope
D: Owner's Manual
E: Silver Polishing Cloth
F: Alcohol Swab
G: Cotton Fiber Cloth
H: Cleaning Rod
I: Name Tag
J: Micro fiber Cloth

 **KAKULIN musical instruments co.**

service@kakulin.com

Copyrighted Work by:
Patamù
Opera filed on: 13 August 2015
Register No.23229
License type: All rights reserved

ISBN: 978-1-911424-09-3
ISMN: 979-0-9002358-3-1

SKU/ID: 9781911424093

Publishing Company:
Black Wolf Edition & Publishing Ltd..
2 Glebe Place Burntisland KY3 0ES, Scotland
www.blackwolfedition.com

Copyright © 2016 by Black Wolf Edition & Publishing Ltd.
All rights reserved. - First Printing: 2016

© 2016 BWEP

www.ingramcontent.com/pod-product-compliance
Lightning Source LLC
Chambersburg PA
CBHW042016090526
44587CB00028B/4276